Exam FA1
Recording Financial Transactions

Pocket Notes

KAPLAN
PUBLISHING

British library cataloguing-in-publication data

A catalogue record for this book is available from the British Library.

Published by:
Kaplan Publishing UK
Unit 2 The Business Centre
Molly Millars Lane
Wokingham
Berkshire
RG41 2QZ

ISBN 978-1-83996-154-0

© Kaplan Financial Limited, 2022

Printed and bound in Great Britain.

The text in this material and any others made available by any Kaplan Group company does not amount to advice on a particular matter and should not be taken as such. No reliance should be placed on the content as the basis for any investment or other decision or in connection with any advice given to third parties. Please consult your appropriate professional adviser as necessary. Kaplan Publishing Limited and all other Kaplan group companies expressly disclaim all liability to any person in respect of any losses or other claims, whether direct, indirect, incidental, consequential or otherwise arising in relation to the use of such materials.

All rights reserved. No part of this publication may be reproduced, stored in a retrieval system, or transmitted, in any form or by any means, electronic, mechanical, photocopying, recording or otherwise, without the prior written permission of Kaplan Publishing.

Contents

Chapter 1	Business transactions	1
Chapter 2	Double-entry bookkeeping	9
Chapter 3	Sales and sales records	19
Chapter 4	Purchases and purchase records	33
Chapter 5	Recording receipts and payments	45
Chapter 6	Petty cash	59
Chapter 7	Payroll	67
Chapter 8	Bank reconciliations	75
Chapter 9	Control accounts	79
Chapter 10	The trial balance	89
Index		I.1

Preface

These Pocket Notes contain everything you need to know for the exam, presented in a unique visual way that makes revision easy and effective.

Written by experienced lecturers and authors, these Pocket Notes break down content into manageable chunks to maximise your concentration.

Quality and accuracy are of the utmost importance to us so if you spot an error in any of our products, please send an email to mykaplanreporting@kaplan.com with full details, or follow the link to the feedback form in MyKaplan.

Our Quality Co-ordinator will work with our technical team to verify the error and take action to ensure it is corrected in future editions.

Introduction

In this chapter

- Overview of the examination.
- Keys syllabus areas.

Overview of the examination

The examination is a two-hour computer-based examination. It will comprise 50 two-mark compulsory multiple-choice questions.

As the examination is multiple choice only, you do need to consider the following:

- Multiple choice questions allow the examiner to cover a significant amount of the syllabus within each examination. This means you cannot simply learn only part of the syllabus and hope to achieve a pass standard – you will need to learn the entire syllabus to maximise your chances of success in the examination.

- Your question practice must be focused on multiple choice questions. As part of your revision, work through the questions in the study text and any question banks you may have to ensure you understand the style of question asked.

- Remember in the examination, you can answer questions in any order. It is therefore worth completing the easier questions first and then re-visiting the more difficult questions at the end of the examination. This approach will (hopefully) ensure you have obtained the easy marks first and avoid missing this should you run out of time.

- The multiple-choice questions will include both computational and non-computational elements.

Finally, when all else fails guess – there is no negative marking.

Key syllabus areas

- Business transactions and documentation
- Double entry bookkeeping
- Banking and petty cash
- Sales and sales records
- Purchases and purchase records
- Payroll
- Control accounts and the initial trial balance

chapter 1

Business transactions

In this chapter

- Types of business.
- Accounting systems.
- Cash transactions.
- Key documents in credit sales / purchases systems.
- Other business documents.

Types of business

Types of business

Sole trader
- One person owns/runs business
- Entitled to all profit
- Suffers all loss
- Owners liable for business debts
- May have employees

Partnership
- Two or more people own/run business
- Profit split between partners according to their agreement
- Partners liable for business debts
- May have employees

Limited company
- Owners = shareholders
- Managers run the business
- Owners have limited liability – not liable for business debts
- In small company, shareholders may = managers

Chapter 1

Accounting systems

Payroll

Purchases
Goods or service obtained from supplier
Can be cash (paid for immediately) or credit (delay between receiving goods/service and payment being made)

Major business accounting systems

Sales
Goods or service provided to customer
Can be cash (paid for immediately) or credit (delay between providing goods/service and payment being received)

Petty Cash

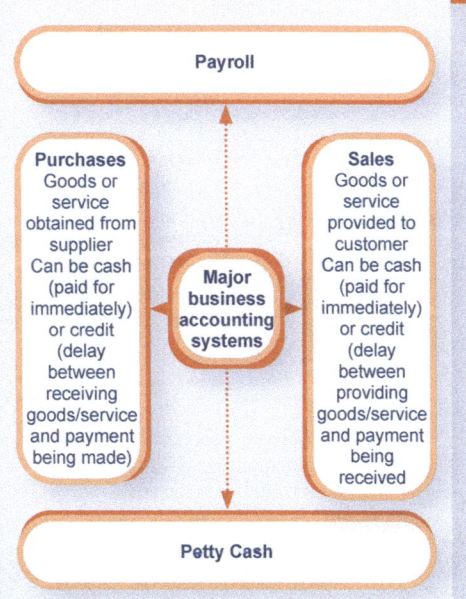

Key Point

- Accounting system used to record transactions.
- Many employees using accounting systems / ledger accounts.
- Control system therefore in place to ensure complete and accurate recording of transactions.

Reasons for producing business documents

- Evidence of the transaction and its details.
- Evidence of the stage that a transaction has reached (e.g. delivery note shows goods received).
- Check and confirm transactions made.
- Recording transaction details.

Business transactions

Cash transactions

Types of business

1. Over the counter sale
Cash or credit sale in shop. Customer given receipt to confirm transaction

2. Verbal order
Goods not yet available – order details written down on sales form for delivery when goods in stock

3. Telephone order
Order recorded on sales order form by company /goods dispatched to customer

4. Written order
Order form completed by customer – sent to company. Goods dispatched to customer

5. Internet order
Customer completes electronic order form on web site. May make payment on secure site. Goods sent to customer

Cheque requisitions

Situations

For abnormal expenses or payment requests not supported by invoice, e.g.

- deposit for catering services
- servicing of company car
- settlement of company credit card.

Process

1. Cheque requisition form completed by manager and any supporting documentation attached.
2. Authorised by head of department.
3. Sent to cashier.
4. Cheque drawn up.

Key Point

Credit transactions

- Sales/purchases made with payment made later.
- Credit terms agreed – amount of time before payment is required and maximum amount of credit.
- Terms set by credit controller.
- Individual large orders may have own credit terms.

Business transactions

Key documents in credit sales/purchases systems

Sales system

- **Sales order**: Customer purchase order acts as a request to sell goods to that customer
- **Delivery note**: Sent to customer with goods – copy retained at company
- **Sales invoice**: Generated from delivery note – details of sale made and request for payment
- **Remittance advice**: From customer with payment listing sales invoices paid

Purchase system

- **Purchase requisition**: Request for goods – counter signed by authorised person
- **Purchase order**: Official order sent to supplier
- **Delivery note**: Sent from supplier with goods
- **Purchase invoice**: Sent from supplier detailing goods supplied and price. Acts as request for payment
- **Payment**: Sent to supplier along with remittance advice
- **Goods received note**: Details copied from delivery note (Check details)

Documents – essential contents

Sales invoices/Purchase invoices

- Customer name and address
- Name of business, business address and telephone number
- Invoice number
- Invoice date
- Customer account reference
- Order number
- Goods: quantity, description, price
- Total invoice value
- Settlement terms

Purchase orders

- Business name of buyer
- Registered office and company registration number
- Supplier name and address
- Purchase order number
- Business contact
- Delivery date

Key Point

- Sales invoice sent from company to customer for goods supplied.
- Purchase invoice received from a company for goods purchased.

Business transactions

Other business documents

Statement of account
Sent monthly to customer showing invoices not yet paid

Credit note
Sent from supplier to customer, cancels part or whole of invoice for goods returned

Debit note
A document raised by a customer and issued to a supplier to request a credit note.

Petty cash voucher
Shows authorised expenditure from petty cash supported by documentation showing expense is genuine

Employee payslip
Notification to employee of wages earned less statutory and other authorised deductions

Contents of the payslip:

- employee's / employer's name
- date
- total gross pay split into elements e.g overtime, etc
- any employee pension contribution
- deductions from, or adjustments to, pay
- total gross pay to date
- total tax paid to date in tax year and tax due this pay day
- National Insurance/social security contributions due this pay day
- net pay.

Exam focus

Remember many of the multiple-choice questions on this section are factual so ensure you remember the names of the different types of business documents and what each is used for.

chapter 2

Double-entry bookkeeping

In this chapter

- The accounting equation.
- Income, expenses and profit.
- Accounts and ledgers.
- Books of prime entry.
- Double-entry bookkeeping.
- Balancing accounts.
- Capital and revenue expenditure.
- Computerised accounting.

Double-entry bookkeeping

The accounting equation

Key Point

The accounting equation shows relationship between assets and liabilities in accounting system.

Definition

Business entity concept: A business is separate from its owners.

Any business always has:

- Assets – resources controlled
- Liabilities – amounts owed to third parties
- Capital – money introduced by owners

Assets
- Land and buildings
- Plant and machinery
- Motor vehicles
- Inventory
- Money in bank
- Receivables

=

Liabilities
- Payables
- Bank loan
- Bank overdraft
- Other payables (e.g. tax due to tax authorities)

+

Capital
- Amounts introduced to business by owner

- Elements change over time (e.g. when a sale occurs stock will fall and money in bank-increase)

Assets
- $2,000 Land
- $3,000 Inventory
- $1,500 – Money in the bank
- Total $5,500

=

Liabilities
- $1,500 due to payables

+

Capital
- $4,000 capital from owner

Income, expenses and profit

- Businesses sell goods and services

Definition

- Income = amounts received for selling goods and services
- Expenses = amounts paid to provide those goods and services
- Profit = excess of income over expenditure. Added to owner's capital (or deducted if a loss)

Key Point

Every transaction has two effects (the dual aspect). This means that after each transaction the accounting equation will still balance.

Income
- Sales of goods/services

−

Expenses
- Cost of materials used
- Salaries
- Telephone charges
- Rent
- Light, heat and power
- Interest on bank loan

=

Profit
- Surplus of sales over expenses paid
- Can be negative – indicates loss

Double-entry bookkeeping

Accounts and ledgers

- An account is kept for each asset, liability, income and expense item.
- Each account is given a code number.
- Accounts are kept together in the nominal ledger.
- Nominal ledger also known as main or general ledger.
- Each transaction is recorded once as a Debit and once as a Credit in two separate accounts in nominal ledger.

Account name and code			
Date and reference	$	Date and reference	$
Debits		**Credits**	

Definition

Ledger = set of related accounts

Books of prime entry

Use	Examples
- Books where individual transactions are first recorded in a company - Totalled periodically and totals transferred to nominal ledger - Transfer journal used to record less frequent transactions (e.g. write off irrecoverable debts, correction of errors)	- Sales day book (credit sales) - Purchase day book (credit purchases) - Cash book (bank receipts and payments) - Petty cash book (cash payments) - Transfer journal

Double-entry bookkeeping

A decrease in any balance is shown on the opposite side of account e.g. decrease in asset will be a credit entry.

Example

Purchase of motor vehicle:

- Debit motor vehicles account (increasing asset).
- Credit bank (decreasing the asset bank with the payment made).

Exam focus

Ensure that you are confident with which balances are debits and which are credits.

Questions focus on this.

Nominal ledger – recording of assets and liabilities

Increase in debits	Increase in credits
Assets	Liabilities
Expenses	Income
	Owner's capital

Bank

	Motor vehicle 10,000

Motor vehicles

Bank account 10,000	

Double-entry bookkeeping

Balancing accounts

- Accounts closed ('ruled off') occasionally – each month or year.
- 'Balance' on account is carried forward to the next accounting period.
- Where debits > credits, account has a debit balance.
- Where credits > debits, account has a credit balance.

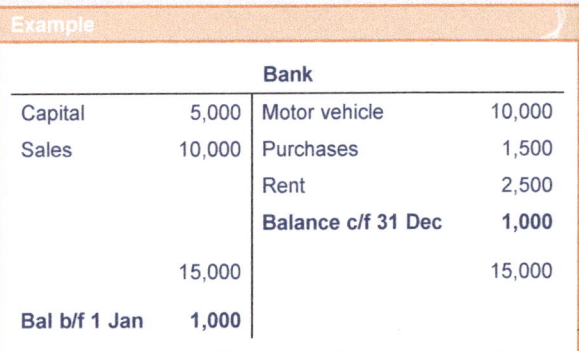

Example

Bank

Capital	5,000	Motor vehicle	10,000
Sales	10,000	Purchases	1,500
		Rent	2,500
		Balance c/f 31 Dec	**1,000**
	15,000		15,000
Bal b/f 1 Jan	1,000		

- Debit entries total $15,000; credit entries total $14,000
- Subtotals are made equal at higher amount of $15,000
- Balancing figure of $1,000 is inserted on credit side of account
- This is carried forward to become a debit balance at the start of the next accounting period

Capital and revenue expenditure

Definition

- **Capital expenditure** refers to the purchase of assets for long-term use in the business (>1 year).
- **Revenue expenditure** is expenditure on expense items / goods for resale.

Capital expenditure may also be referred to as asset expenditure. Revenue expenditure may also be referred to as an expense.

Definition

- Assets for long-term use in the business are **non-current assets**.
- Assets for short-term use in the business are **current assets**. They include inventory, cash and receivables.

Computerised accounting

Computerised bookkeeping uses same principles as manual bookkeeping. Double entry still performed – although printouts unlikely to be in 'T' account format.

Advantages of computers	Disadvantages of computers
- Speed - Work from stored programs – needs fewer staff - Reliable – fewer mistakes than manual systems - Can be programmed to undertake complex decision making - Large amounts of data can be stored in very little space and retrieved quickly	- Lack of intelligence – cannot recognise errors or incomplete data - Relatively high initial costs - More difficult to amend computer programs than manual system - Makes organisation dependent on computer – more vulnerable to loss of resource - Can only make quantifiable not judgemental decisions

Integrated accounting packages

Cash book systems	Electronic version of manual cash book
Basic bookkeeping systems	Basic sales, purchase and nominal ledgers + ability to produce sales tax returns, TBs and financial statements
Bookkeeping and accounting systems	As a basic bookkeeping system but with credit/inventory control facilities

Coding systems

All accounts should be given a code.

Sequential codes	Codes allocated in numerical order	0001 property 0002 motor vehicles
Faceted codes	Each digit signifies unit of information	3401: 3 = canned food 4 = soup 01 = Heinz
Mnemonic / significant digit codes	Codes include descriptive element off account in question	502828 – Jeans – 28" waist, 28" leg 503028 – Jeans – 30" waist, 28" leg
Block /hierarchical codes	Numerical blocks of codes allocated to certain types of accounts	0000 – 0999 non-current assets 1000 – 1999 current assets

Features of a good coding system:

- each item has unique code
- codes of uniform length/make up
- codes are significant
- index of codes exists
- scope for additional codes
- characters (commas, colons, etc) not used
- new codes authorised.

Exam focus

This section introduced the concept of double-entry bookkeeping. If you need to practise setting up 'T' accounts, please refer to the examples in the study text.

chapter
3

Sales and sales records

In this chapter

- Sales invoices and credit notes.
- Sales tax.
- Discounts.
- Variable consideration.
- Stages in preparing a sales invoice.
- Recording a sales invoice.
- Recording sales returns.
- Statements of account.
- Aged receivables analysis.
- Communications with customers.
- Irrecoverable debts.

Sales invoices and credit notes

- For credit notes – obtain reason for credit and ensure goods returned prior to issuing credit.
- Credit note will also decrease amount of sales tax payable.

Sales tax

Overview	VAT (sales tax) invoice
• Sales tax is a tax on the ultimate consumer	• Sales tax registration number
• Collected by businesses on behalf of government	• Tax point – date of transaction for sales tax purposes
• Charge sales tax on sales price	• Rate of sales tax
• Pays sales tax on purchases	• Amount of sales tax charged
• Sales tax charged at 20% (UK)	

Chapter 3

Sales invoice

Copies sent
- To customer – acts as record of goods purchased and reminder for payment
- To accounts dept – to update Sales Day Book
- To file for reference in case of dispute

Settlement terms
- Net 30 days – due within 30 days
- E & O E = errors and omissions excepted – can amend invoice if wrong later
- Ex works = customer pays for delivery

Contents of
- See Chapter 1 plus:
- Sales tax amount
- Sales tax number of organisation
- Tax point

Cancelled by →

Credit invoice

Purpose
- Cancels part or all of invoice
- Used where invoice already sent out

Contents of
- As invoice plus:
- States is a credit note
- Gives reason for credit
- Shows clearly goods being credited

Reasons for
- Customer returns damaged goods
- Customer returns goods not ordered
- Customer does not receive goods
- Correct invoicing error

Discounts

Trade discounts	Settlement discounts
Given to:	Given to:
• Regular customers	• Credit customers
• Customers buying in bulk	
• Given at point of sale	• Given if payment received within stated time
• Calculated on price net of sales tax	
• Sales tax then calculated on price after discount given	

Variable consideration

When goods are sold on credit, the seller must estimate the amount of revenue that will be receivable. Trade discount is always deducted in arriving at the price to be invoiced. If early settlement terms are offered to the customer, the seller must estimate whether or not it is probable that the early settlement terms offered will be taken by the customer.

If it is probable that early settlement will be made by the customer, then early settlement discount should be deducted in arriving at the invoice price.

If it is probable that early settlement will not be made by the customer, early settlement discount is not deducted in arriving at the invoice price.

When cash is subsequently received from the customer, any under- or over-receipt of cash (in comparison with the receivable recorded) is adjusted against revenue.

> **Example**
>
> A business sold goods to a customer on credit at a list price of $240. Early settlement discount of 4% was offered to the customer for payment within 7 days of invoice date.
>
> If the customer is expected to take advantage of the settlement discount offered, the revenue and receivable will be recorded as: $240 × 96% = $230.40.
>
> If the customer is not expected to take advantage of the settlement discount offered, the revenue and receivable will be recorded as $240.

Sales and sales records

Example

A business sold goods with a list price of $120 and offered a 5% trade discount to the customer. Sales tax is charged at 20%.

Net value of sales invoice $120 × 95% = $114

Sales tax: 20% × $114 = $22.80

Gross value of sales invoice:

$114 + $22.80 = $136.80

Exam focus

Exam questions often give you tax inclusive and exclusive amounts and require you to calculate the tax amount. Make sure that you are comfortable with calculations based on net and gross amounts.

Stages in preparing a sales invoice

Authorisation: Relevant manager authorises preparation of invoice after goods/services provided

Preparation: Customer details: E.g. name, address and discount terms

Preparation: Goods details: Full description of goods sold including price

Checking: Checked against original documents (order etc) for accuracy

Sales invoices also coded with additional data, often a grid box stamp.

Code	Example	Reason
Main ledger account	5003	Show which ledger account sale posted to
Additions and calculations checked	✓	Confirm accuracy of invoice
Sales ledger account number	J8762	Ensure invoice posted to correct customer account
Initial when posted	RGG	Confirm invoice posted to nominal and sales ledger

Sales and sales records

Recording a sales invoice

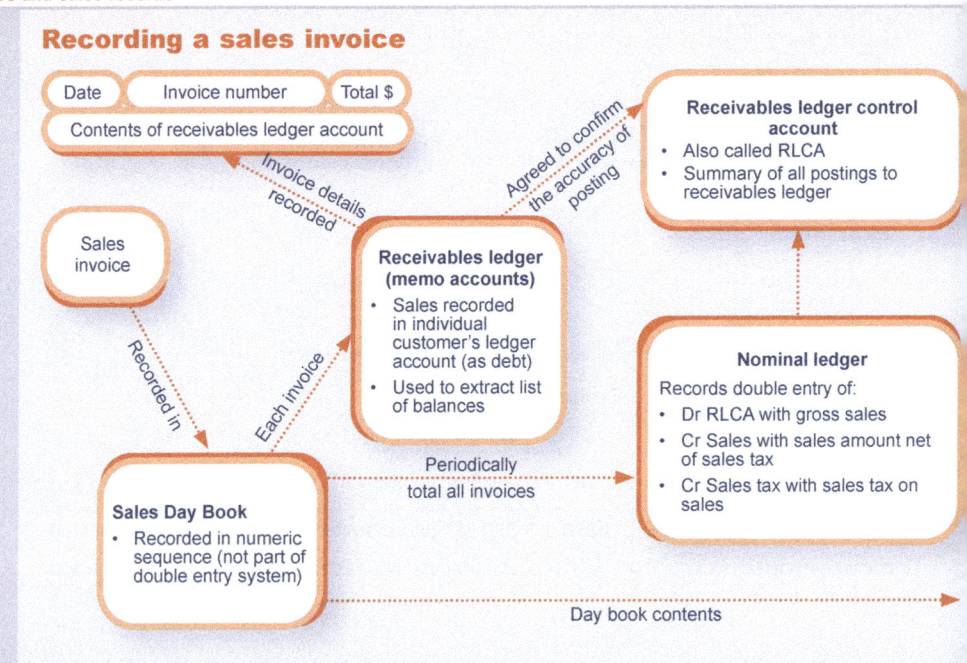

Sales invoice

Recorded in → **Sales Day Book**
- Recorded in numeric sequence (not part of double entry system)

Invoice details recorded → Date | Invoice number | Total $ | Contents of receivables ledger account

Each invoice → **Receivables ledger (memo accounts)**
- Sales recorded in individual customer's ledger account (as debt)
- Used to extract list of balances

Periodically total all invoices → **Nominal ledger**
Records double entry of:
- Dr RLCA with gross sales
- Cr Sales with sales amount net of sales tax
- Cr Sales tax with sales tax on sales

Agreed to confirm the accuracy of posting → **Receivables ledger control account**
- Also called RLCA
- Summary of all postings to receivables ledger

Day book contents →

26 KAPLAN PUBLISHING

Contents of Sales Day Book

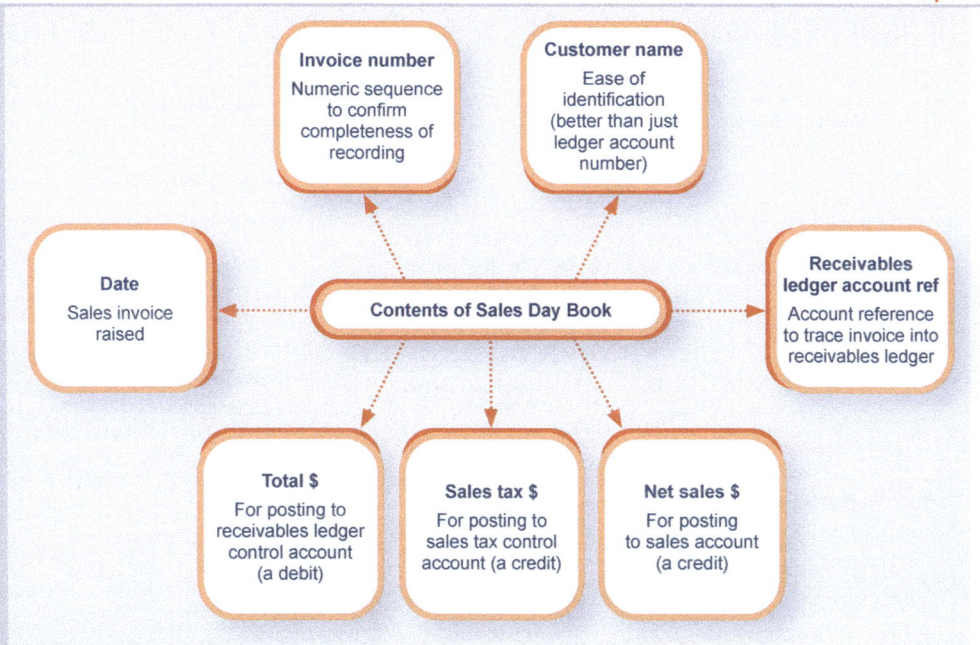

- **Invoice number**: Numeric sequence to confirm completeness of recording
- **Customer name**: Ease of identification (better than just ledger account number)
- **Receivables ledger account ref**: Account reference to trace invoice into receivables ledger
- **Date**: Sales invoice raised
- **Total $**: For posting to receivables ledger control account (a debit)
- **Sales tax $**: For posting to sales tax control account (a credit)
- **Net sales $**: For posting to sales account (a credit)

Sales and sales records

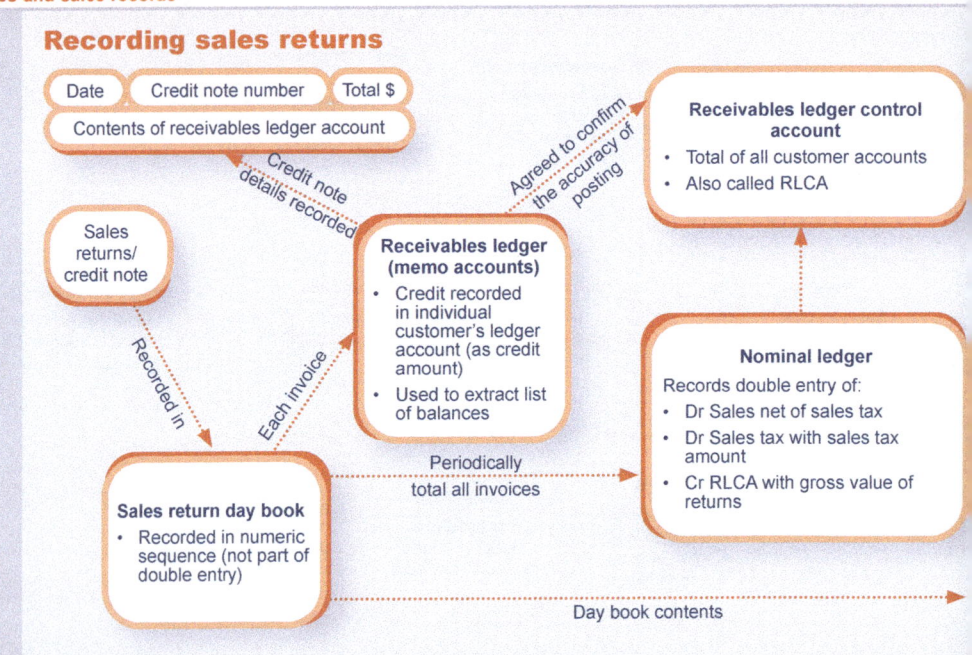

Recording sales returns

- Date
- Credit note number
- Total $
- Contents of receivables ledger account

Sales returns/credit note
- Recorded in Sales return day book
- Credit note details recorded in Receivables ledger (memo accounts)

Receivables ledger (memo accounts)
- Credit recorded in individual customer's ledger account (as credit amount)
- Used to extract list of balances

Sales return day book
- Recorded in numeric sequence (not part of double entry)
- Periodically total all invoices → Nominal ledger

Nominal ledger
Records double entry of:
- Dr Sales net of sales tax
- Dr Sales tax with sales tax amount
- Cr RLCA with gross value of returns

Receivables ledger control account
- Total of all customer accounts
- Also called RLCA

Agreed to confirm the accuracy of posting

Day book contents

Contents of sales return day book

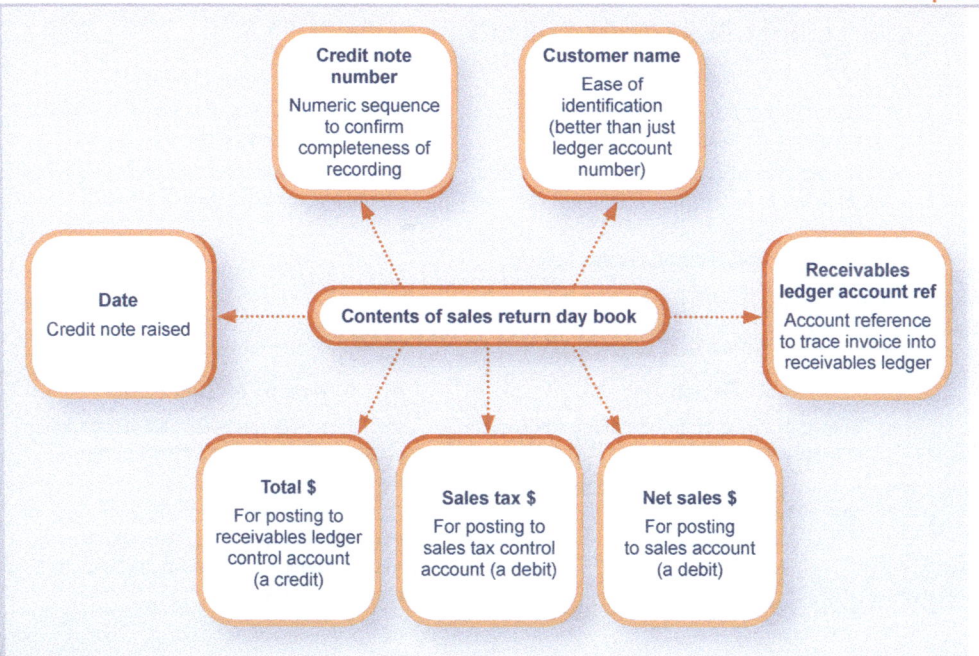

- **Credit note number**: Numeric sequence to confirm completeness of recording
- **Customer name**: Ease of identification (better than just ledger account number)
- **Receivables ledger account ref**: Account reference to trace invoice into receivables ledger
- **Date**: Credit note raised
- **Total $**: For posting to receivables ledger control account (a credit)
- **Sales tax $**: For posting to sales tax control account (a debit)
- **Net sales $**: For posting to sales account (a debit)

Statements of account

Explanation	Reason for producing
- Statement of transactions with one customer since last statement date - Shows balance b/f, all transactions (sales, returns, cash payments, etc.) and balance c/f - Extracted from individual sales ledger accounts	- Remind customers of state of their account (and request payment) - Record for customers of items purchased to check against their own records

Aged receivables analysis

Explanation	Reason for producing
- Shows analysis of amounts due from each individual receivable - Amount split by age of invoice (e.g. 0 to 30 days, 31 to 60 days…)	- Identifies customers with old outstanding balances for additional credit control procedures - Shows total aged receivable by month for management reporting. This identifies to management how efficient credit control procedures are

Communications with customers

Provision of credit	Setting credit limits	Chasing overdue debts
• Encourages sales • Ensures business remains competitive **Costs include:** • Funding working capital • Extra accounting system / staff • Performing credit checks • Operating a credit control function • Cost of customer defaulting • Legal costs of chasing debt	Limits based on: • Bank references • Supplier references • Creditworthiness computer programs • Interview with customer	Procedures include: • Send reminder letter • Speak to customer on telephone • Send final reminder letter • Refer to debt collection agency or solicitor

Irrecoverable debts

Irrecoverable debts are sometimes called bad debts. However, this is now old terminology.

- Amount due from customers unlikely to be paid.
- Main reason for – customer bankrupt.
- Recognise in accounts by removing the receivable balance and increase the irrecoverable debt expense account.
- Requires correct authorisation as debt removed from company's books.
- Relief for any unpaid sales tax may also be available.

Key Point

Remember to update the individual customer account in the sales ledger.

Irrecoverable debts expense account

SLCA 2,500	

RLCA

	Irrecoverable debt 2,500

chapter 4

Purchases and purchase records

In this chapter

- Ordering system.
- Checking purchase invoices and credit notes.
- Authorising and coding of purchase invoices.
- Recording purchases.
- Recording purchase returns.
- Balancing supplier accounts.
- Supplier statements.
- Aged payables analysis.
- Communications with suppliers.

Purchases and purchase records

Ordering system

Stages in ordering goods to obtaining purchase invoice.

Purchase requisition
- Purchase approved by responsible official.
- Normally a manual document
- Results in purchase order being produced – possible after quotes obtained from supplier

Purchase order
- Written request to supply specified goods/services
- May be issued by specialist purchasing department in large organisation

Supply of goods
- Supplier sends goods with delivery note (DN)
- Checked against goods to ensure DN and goods agree
- If reject goods, note on both copies of DN (one at company and one returned to supplier)

Supply of services
- Some form of documentary evidence provided e.g. timesheet to support work carried out

Purchase invoice
- Normally sent to accounts department
- Shows quantity and price of goods delivered

Sales tax on purchase invoice

Check correct sales tax rate used and supplier's sales tax registration number on invoice. Settlement discount offered – ensure sales tax calculated on goods value net of discount.

Chapter 4

Checking purchase invoices and credit notes

Checks carried out – supply of goods
- Invoice agrees to purchase order
- Invoice agrees to goods received
- Correct prices charged on invoice

Treatment in accounts department
- Invoice, purchase order and delivery note matched and filed together
- Unmatched invoices, purchase orders etc filed separately awaiting other matching documents

Checks carried out
- Arithmetical accuracy
- Ensure for correct amount by comparison with original invoice

Purpose
- Cancels part or all of invoice
- Easier than amending invoice (already recorded in SDB of supplying company)

Checks carried out – supply of services
- Invoice agrees to purchase order
- Invoice agrees to supporting documentation e.g. timesheet
- Correct prices charged and invoice casts correctly
- Lack of documentation – check invoice is 'reasonable' e.g. utility bill

Purchase invoice — Amended by → **Credit note (from supplier)**

Contents of
- See Chapter 1 plus:
- sales tax amount
- sales tax number of supplying organisation

Contents of
As invoice plus:
- States is a credit note
- Gives reason for credit
- Shows clearly goods being credited

Reasons for
- Return damaged goods
- Returns goods not ordered
- Invoice received but not goods
- Purchase invoice errors

Purchases and purchase records

Authorising and coding of purchase invoices

Methods of authorisation	Coding
1 Purchase invoice agreed to supporting documentation (e.g. GRN and Purchase Order) 2 Purchase invoice sent to official authorising expenditure, then signed by that person confirming invoice correct	All invoices coded with: • Nominal ledger code – ensure asset and expense differentiated • Supplier code for posting to payables ledger control account

Purchase invoices also:

- Given sequential number to assist completeness of recording.
- Should have checklist attached to confirm all checks (e.g. agreed to purchase order) have been performed.
- Checklist may take time form of a grid box stamp.

Chapter 4

Recording purchases

Purchase invoice — Recorded in → **Purchase Day Book**
- Recorded in numeric sequence (not part of double entry system)

Contents of payables ledger account: Date | Invoice number | Total $

Each invoice → **Payables ledger (memo accounts)**
- Purchase recorded in individual supplier's ledger account (as credit)

Invoice details recorded ← Payables ledger

Periodically total all invoices → **Nominal ledger**
Records double entry of:
- Dr Expense accounts with net purchase amount
- Dr sales tax control with sales tax amount
- CR PLCA with gross purchase amounts

Payables ledger control account
- Summary of all postings to payables ledger
- Also called PLCA

Agreed to confirm the accuracy of posting

Day book contents → Nominal ledger

Purchases and purchase records

Contents of Purchase Day Book

- **Invoice number**: Numeric sequence to confirm completeness of recording
- **Supplier name**: Ease of identification (better than just ledger account number)
- **Supplier code**: Account reference to trace invoice into payables ledger
- **Net purchase $**: Analysed by type of purchase ready for posting to expense accounts in nominal ledger (a debit)
- **Sales tax $**: For posting to sales tax control account (a debit)
- **Total $**: For posting to Payables Ledger Control Account (a credit)
- **Date**: On purchase invoice

Chapter 4

Recording purchase returns

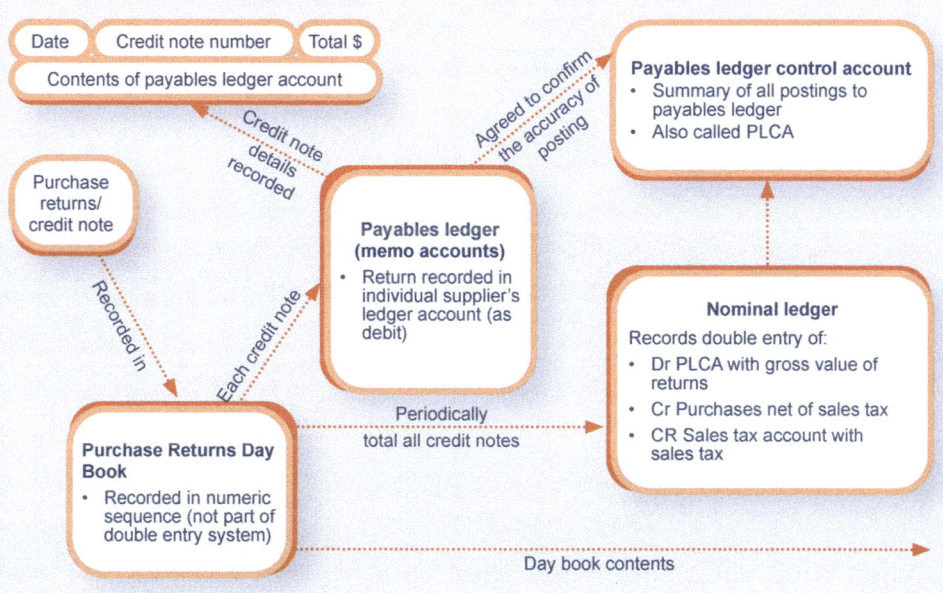

Purchase Returns Day Book entry columns:
- Date
- Credit note number
- Total $
- Contents of payables ledger account

Purchase returns/credit note → Recorded in → **Purchase Returns Day Book**
- Recorded in numeric sequence (not part of double entry system)

Credit note details recorded → (to day book columns above)

Each credit note → **Payables ledger (memo accounts)**
- Return recorded in individual supplier's ledger account (as debit)

Agreed to confirm the accuracy of posting → **Payables ledger control account**
- Summary of all postings to payables ledger
- Also called PLCA

Periodically total all credit notes → **Nominal ledger**

Records double entry of:
- Dr PLCA with gross value of returns
- Cr Purchases net of sales tax
- CR Sales tax account with sales tax

Day book contents →

KAPLAN PUBLISHING

Purchases and purchase records

Contents of Purchase Returns Day Book

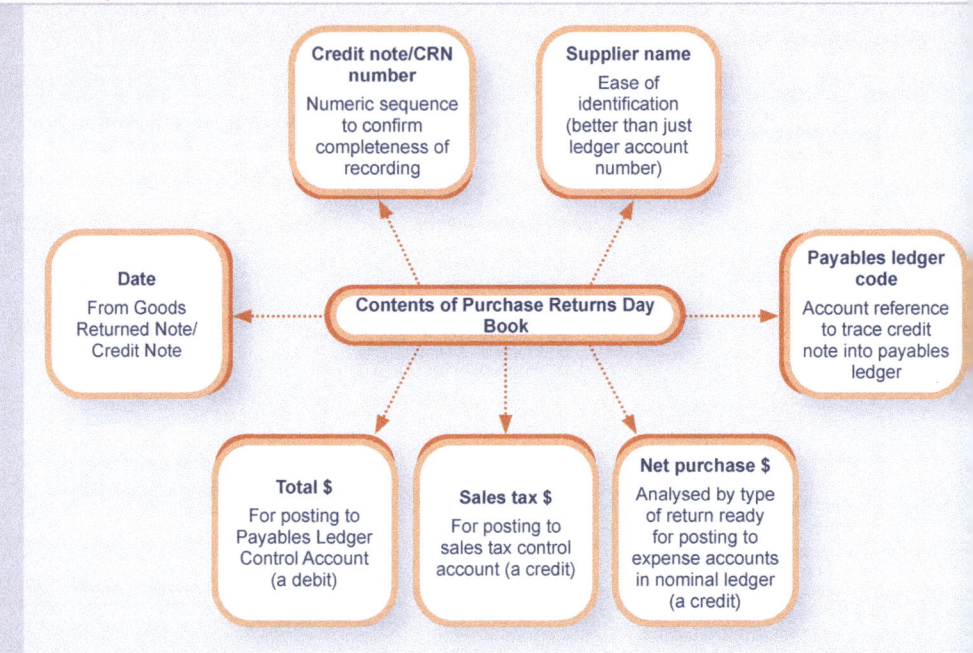

Date
From Goods Returned Note/Credit Note

Credit note/CRN number
Numeric sequence to confirm completeness of recording

Supplier name
Ease of identification (better than just ledger account number)

Payables ledger code
Account reference to trace credit note into payables ledger

Total $
For posting to Payables Ledger Control Account (a debit)

Sales tax $
For posting to sales tax control account (a credit)

Net purchase $
Analysed by type of return ready for posting to expense accounts in nominal ledger (a credit)

Balancing supplier accounts

- Periodically, details of items purchased, payments made, discounts received, etc entered into individual supplier account, as shown right.
- Balance c/f obtained.
- List balances on other supplier accounts and find total amount.
- Agree total to payables ledger control account.
- Check whether all items (especially invoices) have been recorded.
- Check to supplier statement to confirm completeness and accuracy of recording.

ABC Supplies

		Balance b/f 1 Jan	**1,000**
Bank	6,000	PBD	2,400
Discount received	150	PBD	1,500
Balance c/f 31 Jan	**1,000**	PBD	2,250
	7,150		7,150
		Balance b/f 1 Feb	**1,000**

Supplier statements

Key Point

- Received each month from suppliers.
- Shows transactions with their customer (the purchasing company).
- Balance should agree to individual supplier account in payables ledger.
- Supplier statement and ledger balance may not agree due to items such as:
    1. Cash in transit (cheque issued but not yet received at supplier).
    2. Invoices not recorded (goods received but invoice not yet received by customer).
    3. Arithmetical errors.
- Therefore supplier statement reconciliation carried out to identify reconciling items and correct errors.

Aged payables analysis

Explanation	Reason for producing
• Shows analysis of amounts payable to suppliers • Analysis split by number of days each amount is outstanding	• Identify suppliers not paid – ensure paid promptly to maintain good supplier relations • Ensure settlement discounts are being claimed and not missed.

Communications with suppliers

- Communication focused on maintaining good supplier relationships and therefore continued supply of goods.
- Most communications relate to standard of goods received or reconciling supplier statements.

Purchases and purchase records

Exam focus

As with sales, you need to ensure you understand the double entry systems for purchases and returns. Refer to the activities in the study text if you need practice on these areas.

chapter
5

Recording receipts and payments

In this chapter

- Recording receipts.
- Recording receipts – cash book (CB) to nominal ledger.
- Cash payments.
- Bank-customer relationship.
- Clearing of cheques.
- Cheques.
- Credit and debit cards.
- Contactless payments.
- Security of cash/cheques.
- Reimbursement of employee expenses.

Recording receipts

Main sources of receipts:
- Cash and cheques from receivables.
- Cash and cheques from cash sales.
- Bank transfers (BACS) from receivables.
- Credit card receipts from card company.
- Receipts from Internet site.

All entered into cash receipts book as shown on right.

Money received
Check against supporting information
- Cheque to remittance advice
- Credit card to vouchers
- Internet sales to credit card vouchers
- Cash to till roll

Prepare remittance list
- For cheques/cash identifying customer account for each receipt
- Alternatively note receipt as cash sale

Cash and cheques only
- Bank paying-in slip completed
- Cash and cheques taken to bank

BACS transfer
- Money paid direct to company's bank account from receivable
- Also from internet where debit card used

Procedure
- Review bank statement when received to identify BACS transfers
- Identify customer and amounts paid

Cash receipts book
- Enter receipts into cash book – book of prime entry for cash receipts

Chapter 5

Recording receipts – cash book (CB) to nominal ledger

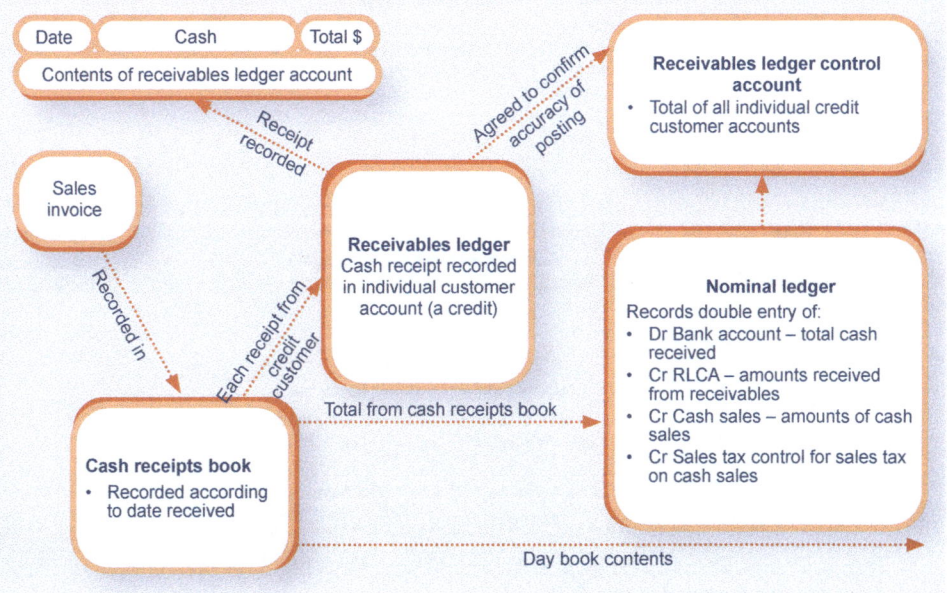

Columns: Date | Cash | Total $
Contents of receivables ledger account

Sales invoice → Recorded in → **Cash receipts book**
- Recorded according to date received

Each receipt from credit customer → **Receivables ledger**
- Cash receipt recorded in individual customer account (a credit)

Receipt recorded (to contents of receivables ledger account)

Agreed to confirm accuracy of posting → **Receivables ledger control account**
- Total of all individual credit customer accounts

Total from cash receipts book → **Nominal ledger**
Records double entry of:
- Dr Bank account – total cash received
- Cr RLCA – amounts received from receivables
- Cr Cash sales – amounts of cash sales
- Cr Sales tax control for sales tax on cash sales

Day book contents (from Cash receipts book to Nominal ledger)

Recording receipts and payments

Contents of cash receipts book:

- **Date**: Date money received
- **Reference**: Either customer code or 'cash sales' if not a credit sale or other applicable reference
- **Customer name**: Ease of identification (better than just ledger account number)
- **Total $**: Total amount of receipt
- **Other income**: E.g. Bank interest received
- **Receivables**: Amount of receipt from receivables
  - Amount from cash sales
- **Sales tax $**: Nothing (sales tax in SDB)
  - Sales tax on cash sales

Note cash sales are assumed to be entered in CB only (not SDB). Sales tax therefore accounted for in the cash book and not the SDB.

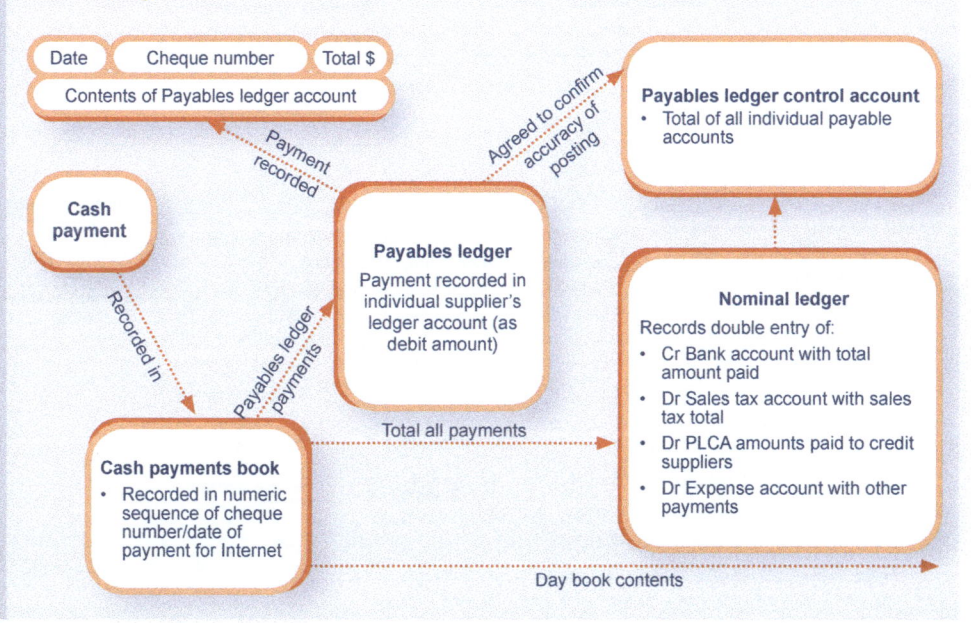

Cash payments

Cash payment

Recorded in → **Cash payments book**
- Recorded in numeric sequence of cheque number/date of payment for Internet

Payables ledger payments → **Payables ledger**
Payment recorded in individual supplier's ledger account (as debit amount)

Payment recorded →
- Date
- Cheque number
- Total $
- Contents of Payables ledger account

Total all payments → **Nominal ledger**
Records double entry of:
- Cr Bank account with total amount paid
- Dr Sales tax account with sales tax total
- Dr PLCA amounts paid to credit suppliers
- Dr Expense account with other payments

Day book contents →

Payables ledger control account
- Total of all individual payable accounts

Agreed to confirm accuracy of posting

Chapter 5

KAPLAN PUBLISHING

Recording receipts and payments

Contents of cash payments book:

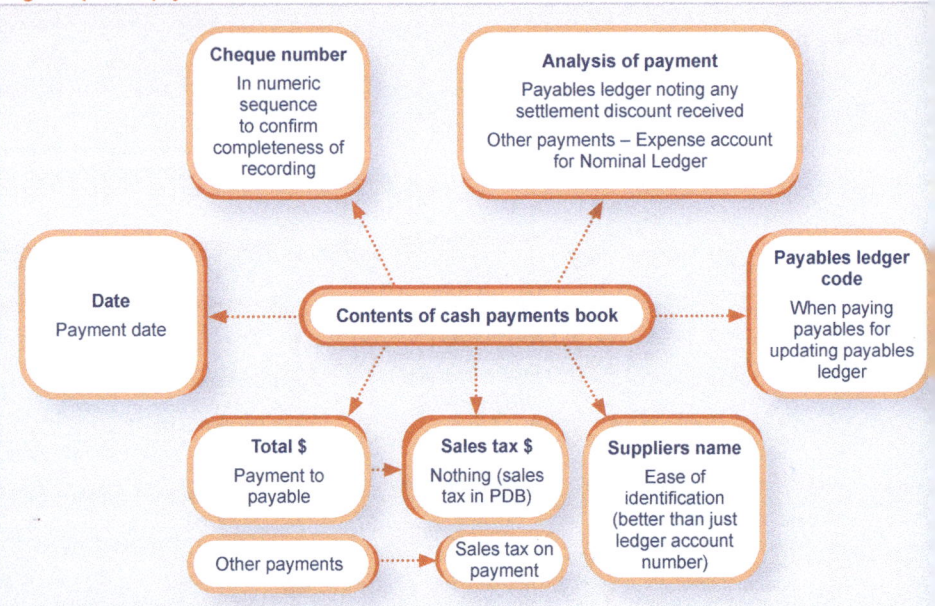

- **Cheque number**: In numeric sequence to confirm completeness of recording
- **Analysis of payment**: Payables ledger noting any settlement discount received. Other payments – Expense account for Nominal Ledger
- **Date**: Payment date
- **Payables ledger code**: When paying payables for updating payables ledger
- **Total $**: Payment to payable
- **Sales tax $**: Nothing (sales tax in PDB)
- **Other payments** → Sales tax on payment
- **Suppliers name**: Ease of identification (better than just ledger account number)

Note: Sales tax is only accounted for on payments not already in the PDB. Invoices recorded in the PDB will already have sales tax accounted for there.

Bank-customer relationship

Bank's obligations	Customer's obligations
• Pay cheques on demand (up to balance in customer's bank account or overdraft limit) • Provide customer with balance on bank accounts • Provide statement showing transactions on bank account • Not to disclose customer information to unauthorised third parties • Use professional care in maintaining customer account	• Exercise reasonable care in drawing up cheques (e.g. not go overdrawn or forge cheques)

Clearing of cheques

Definition

Clearing of cheques is the process of paying in cheque and obtaining money due from that cheque.

1. Cheque paid into local branch of bank.
2. Cheques sent to Head Office.
3. Total amount of cheques due from other 'clearing banks' determined.
4. Net amount due paid to clearing bank's account at Bank of England.
5. Cheques sent to branch drawn on.
6. Drawer's account debited (assuming sufficient funds).
7. Dishonoured cheques returned to drawer.
8. Payee's account credited (following delay for clearing).

This clearing process takes three working days

Exam focus

Ensure that you know banking terminology.

Exam questions may ask what different methods of payment involve.

Cheques

(a) Bank name and branch
(b) Payee – person cheque payable to
(c) & (d) Amount in words and figures
(e) Date cheque written – after six months, bank will treat as out-of-date
(f) Bank sort code – unique to branch
(g) Name of account holder
(h) Account number
(i) Unique cheque number

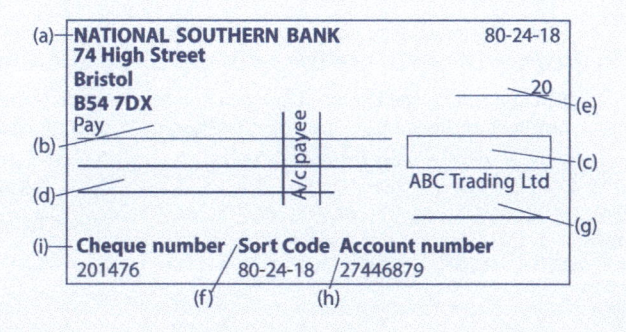

```
(a)— NATIONAL SOUTHERN BANK              80-24-18
     74 High Street
     Bristol
     B54 7DX                                 20    —(e)
     Pay
(b)—_____                      —(c)
                                   ABC Trading Ltd
(d)—_____                      —(g)

(i)— Cheque number  Sort Code  Account number
     201476         80-24-18   27446879
                      (f)        (h)
```

Recording receipts and payments

Cheque terminology	Bank account terminology
'Crossed' – two parallel vertical lines on cheque – payment must be made through bank	**Standing order** – transfer of set amount each month to the same payee
Endorse – pay a third party rather than initial payee – not possible if cheque is crossed	**Direct debit** – third party allowed to take varying amounts from payee, normally monthly
Cheque guarantee cards – bank guarantees payment of cheque up to card limit (cheque must be signed in presence of payee)	**Credit transfer** – Transfer to third party – with amount 'clearing' payee's account at start of transfer
	BACS = Banks Automated Clearing System – system banks use for above payments

Chapter 5

Credit and debit cards

Credit cards

- Customer purchases goods on credit.
- Uses plastic card with magnetic strip or computer chip embedded in card.
- Latter = Chip and pin technology.
- Note charge cards different – full payment must be made each month – no part payments allowed.

Credit card
- Customer pays retailer with card
- Card company sends customer monthly statement
- Customer pays all or part of balance
- Interest paid on outstanding balance
- Card company pays retailer (less commission)

Debit card
- Customer pays retailer with card

Amount transferred from customer's bank account to retailer

TIME

Problems with cheques/credit cards:

Problem	Solution
1. Cheque incorrectly completed by customer	1. Send back to customer for amendment
2. Out-of-date cheque (> six months old)	2. Return to customer for re-issue
3. Credit card limit exceeded	3. Ask customer to pay by different method
4. Payment does not agree with supporting documentation (e.g. underpayment)	4. Inform customer – bank any monies sent and discuss remedial action with customer

Recording receipts and payments

Contactless payments

Contactless payments improve the speed and efficiency of making transactions by eliminating the need to sign a receipt or use a PIN number. The retailer needs to have an appropriate point-of-sale terminal. The customer can request a receipt and can also query the validity of any contactless transaction that appears on their bank or credit card statement.

They tend to be used for low-value transactions to minimise the risk of losses that may be incurred by card issuers or retailers if cards have been inappropriately used.

Security of cash/cheques

- Pay money into bank as soon as possible – minimises risk of fraud and theft.
- Keep cash and cheques in safe when on company premises.
- For large amounts of cash, consider using security firm to bank money – removes risk of individual being robbed on way to bank.

Exam focus

Questions on this area can be factual, e.g. how the banking system works, or more practical requiring knowledge of double-entry bookkeeping. More comprehensive examples of bookkeeping can be found in the study text if you need to revise this further.

Reimbursement of employee expenses

Problems	Solutions
• Claim not authorised in advance • Insufficient supporting evidence, i.e. no receipt provided • Claim exceeds employee's authorised limits	Refer claim to a higher level signatory than is usually the case. They should treat each claim on a case by case basis.

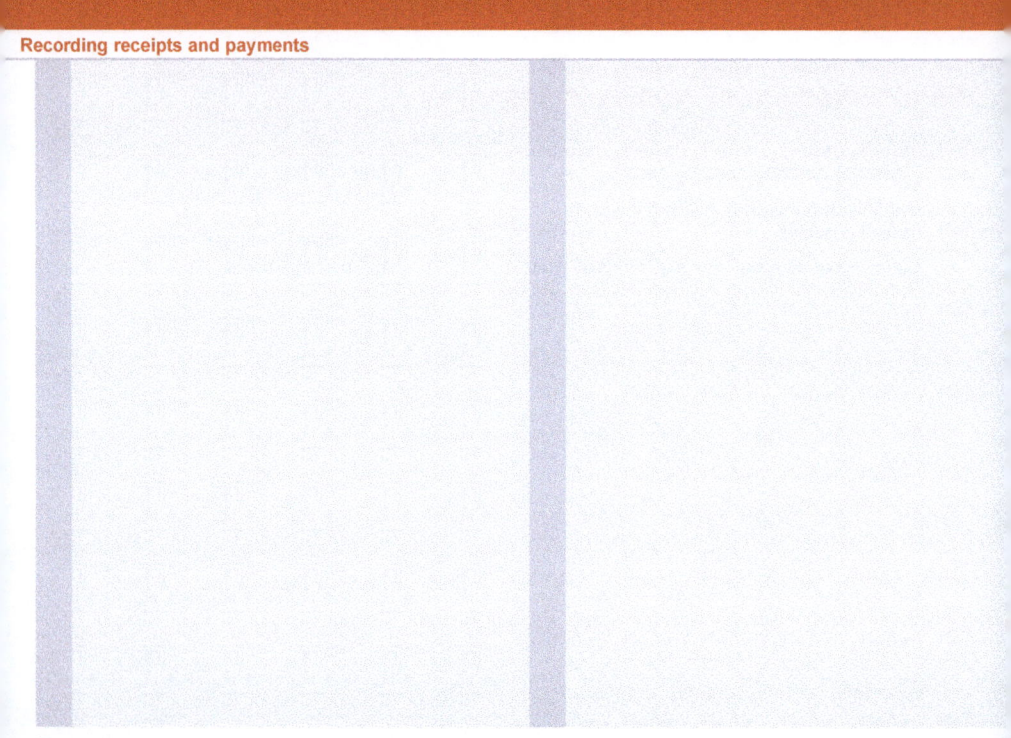

Recording receipts and payments

chapter

6

Petty cash

In this chapter

- Making a petty cash claim.
- Recording of petty cash.
- Reimbursement of petty cash.
- Reconciling petty cash.

Petty cash

Making a petty cash claim

- Normal claim process shown on right.
- Advances can be made – voucher amended to actual amount when receipt obtained – excess money repaid.

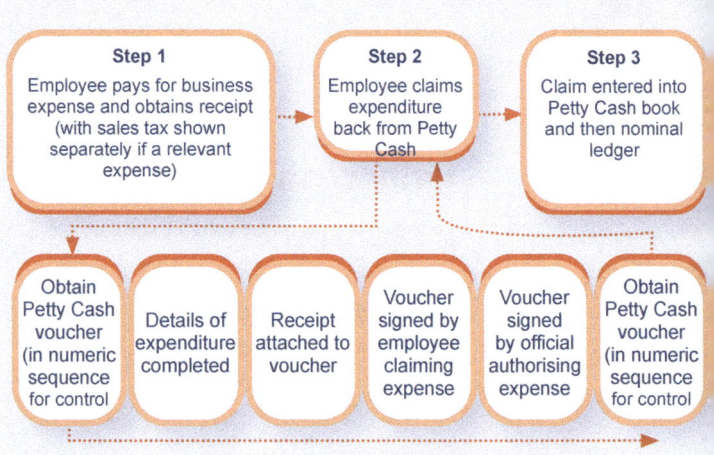

Step 1
Employee pays for business expense and obtains receipt (with sales tax shown separately if a relevant expense)

Step 2
Employee claims expenditure back from Petty Cash

Step 3
Claim entered into Petty Cash book and then nominal ledger

- Obtain Petty Cash voucher (in numeric sequence for control)
- Details of expenditure completed
- Receipt attached to voucher
- Voucher signed by employee claiming expense
- Voucher signed by official authorising expense
- Obtain Petty Cash voucher (in numeric sequence for control)

Authorisation

By
- Petty cashier, or
- Another responsible employee, or
- Petty cashier up to certain limit then another official

Procedure
1. Check amount does not exceed petty cash limits
2. Check claim supported by supporting documentation (sales tax receipt where relevant)

If no supporting documentation available, claim normally approved if 'reasonable'.

Security of petty cash	Problems with petty cash
- Kept in locked petty cash tin, preferably also in locked drawer or safe - Restrictions on number of people with key to tin	- Lack of supporting documentation – allow claim if senior person agrees - Claim exceeds petty cash balance – ask employee to complete standard expense claim

Petty cash

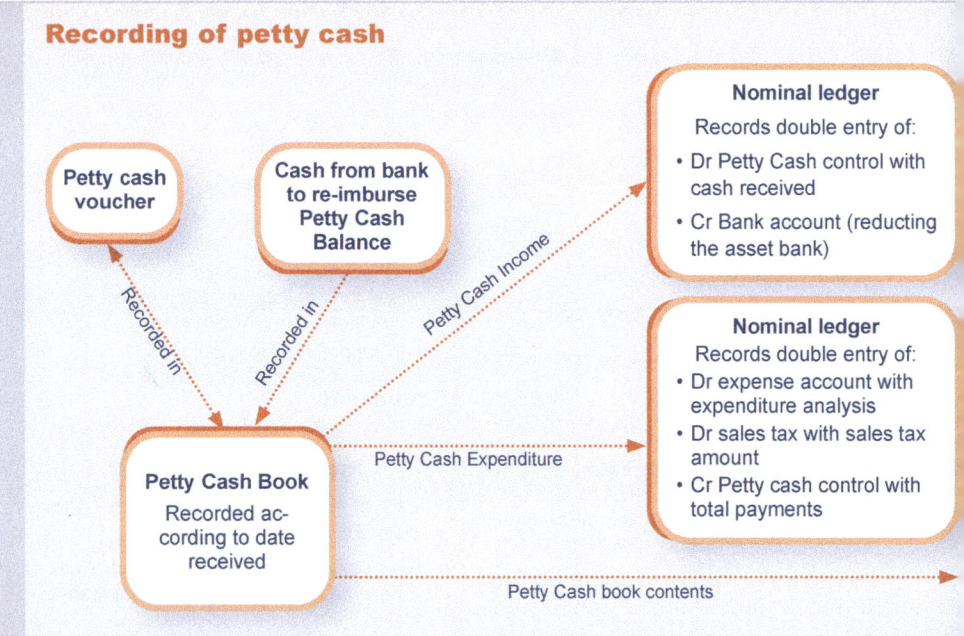

Recording of petty cash

Petty cash voucher — Recorded in → **Petty Cash Book** (Recorded according to date received)

Cash from bank to re-imburse Petty Cash Balance — Recorded in → **Petty Cash Book**

Petty Cash Book — Petty Cash Income → **Nominal ledger**
Records double entry of:
- Dr Petty Cash control with cash received
- Cr Bank account (reducing the asset bank)

Petty Cash Book — Petty Cash Expenditure → **Nominal ledger**
Records double entry of:
- Dr expense account with expenditure analysis
- Dr sales tax with sales tax amount
- Cr Petty cash control with total payments

Petty Cash Book → Petty Cash book contents

Chapter 6

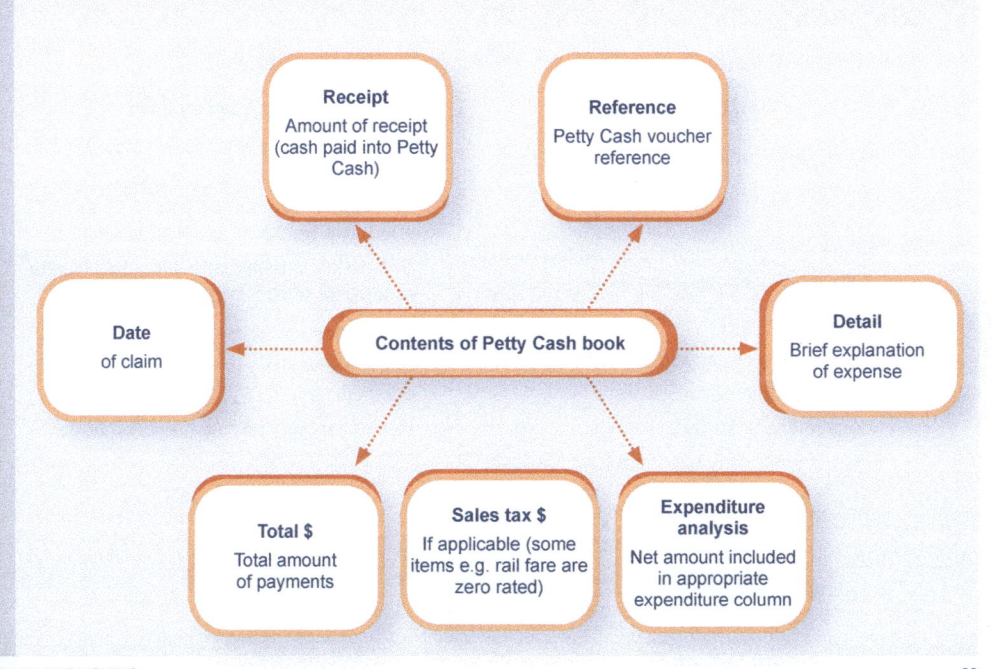

Contents of Petty Cash book

- **Receipt**: Amount of receipt (cash paid into Petty Cash)
- **Reference**: Petty Cash voucher reference
- **Date** of claim
- **Detail**: Brief explanation of expense
- **Total $**: Total amount of payments
- **Sales tax $**: If applicable (some items e.g. rail fare are zero rated)
- **Expenditure analysis**: Net amount included in appropriate expenditure column

Petty cash

Reimbursement of petty cash

Two methods of transferring money from bank account to petty cash account:

Imprest system	Non-imprest system
- Petty cash starts with given amount (e.g. $100) - Expenditure totalled over say two weeks - Exact amount of expenditure added back to petty cash; balance again $100	- Petty cash starts with given amount (e.g. $100) - Expenditure amount estimated as say $75 every two weeks - $75 added to petty cash every two weeks regardless of expenditure
Advantages - Petty cash always returned to same amount - Easy to monitor expenditure - Easy to check for fraud - Warns when petty cash reaching low level	Disadvantages - Large petty cash balance easily accumulates - Petty cash may run out if expenditure consistently underestimated

Reconciling petty cash

Reconciliation	Reason for petty cash not reconciling
• At any time amount of petty cash = imprest balance less total of vouchers / receipts in tin.	• Voucher not same as cash paid out • Incorrect amount of cash paid • Cash stolen

Exam focus

Ensure that you are familiar with the double entry of petty cash and how to calculate the imprest balance on a petty cash account.

Petty cash

chapter 7

Payroll

In this chapter

- Wages/salaries system.
- Basic pay calculations.
- Overtime, bonuses and commission.
- Authorisation and security.
- Accounting for payroll.

Payroll

Wages/salaries system

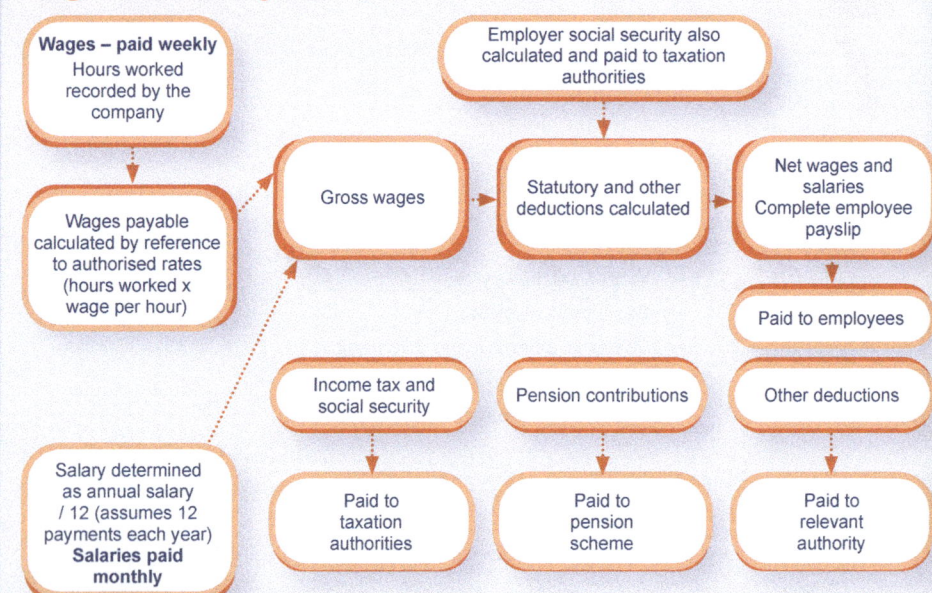

Wages – paid weekly
Hours worked recorded by the company

↓

Wages payable calculated by reference to authorised rates (hours worked × wage per hour)

→ **Gross wages** → Statutory and other deductions calculated → Net wages and salaries Complete employee payslip → Paid to employees

Employer social security also calculated and paid to taxation authorities

Salary determined as annual salary / 12 (assumes 12 payments each year) Salaries paid monthly

Deductions:
- Income tax and social security → Paid to taxation authorities
- Pension contributions → Paid to pension scheme
- Other deductions → Paid to relevant authority

Key points with wages / salary system

- Cost of wages is gross salary + employer's social security (in UK) – other countries may have different regulations.
- Other non-statutory deductions made from gross pay can include:
  - Pension contributions
  - Payroll savings scheme
  - Trade union subscriptions
  - Voluntary deductions e.g. sports club membership.

- Wages / salaries paid by:
  - Cash
  - Cheque, or
  - BACS.

- Employee payslip must contain (by statute):
  - Employer's name
  - Employee's name
  - Date
  - Total gross pay and calculation
  - Employee's pension contributions (if any)
  - Other adjustments to pay
  - Total gross pay to date
  - Total tax paid to date and for this payslip
  - Net pay.

May also contain other information such as payroll number.

Basic pay calculations

Hourly paid employees	Piece rate employees	Salaried employees
Pay = Number of hours worked x hourly rate Hours worked recorded on: • Clock cards • 'Smart' cards • Time sheets	Pay = number of items made x rate per item • Can use differential rates (e.g. higher rate when produce above minimum number of items) • Guaranteed minimum wage – used if piecework wage is lower	Pay = annual salary divided by 12 (monthly pay) or 52 (weekly pay) • Normally paid monthly • Minimum number of hours to work each week, may be eligible for overtime

Overtime, bonuses and commission

Overtime – hourly paid employee	Overtime – salaried employee
• Amount worked over and above 'minimum' hours • Normally calculated at differential rate e.g. time and a half or 150% of the basic wage for overtime worked • Rate may vary depending on overtime hours e.g. 10 + overtime hours at double time	• Amount worked over and above 'minimum' hours • Not all salaried employees are paid overtime – check contract • Hourly rate calculated by dividing annual salary by 52 and then by the number of weekly contracted hours • The contract of employment may override this calculation

Definition

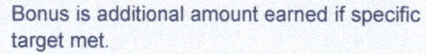

Bonus is additional amount earned if specific target met.

- For example, if output exceeds minimum amount or sales exceed minimum level.
- Paid according to bonus formula e.g. $10 for each unit made above minimum amount.

Definition

Commission amount paid to employee based on that employee's performance.

- Normally paid to sales staff as incentive to make sales.
- Often expressed as % of sales.
- Scheme may contain clause stating amount paid only when customer has paid (not just when sale made).

Authorisation and security

Authorisation	Security

• Authorisation needed for overtime to be worked and then to confirm has been worked
• Authorisation of payroll needed to confirm accuracy of calculation and amounts to be paid
• Authorisation normally:
   – Supervisor signs timesheet
   – Payroll 'signed' by senior accountant
	• Payroll/salary information highly sensitive therefore must be kept secure
	• All information to be kept in locked filing cabinets or secure areas on computer systems
	• Uncollected cash wages to be kept in safe until claimed

- Split of personnel and payroll departments important.
- Compare personnel and payroll department records to identify 'dummy' employees and ensure employees who have left company are no longer paid.

Chapter 7

Accounting for payroll

Gross wages → Calculated

- Salary and wages details recorded each month → • Employer's social security calculated → • Payment made to employees → • Amounts payable to outside agencies e.g. taxation authorities recorded

Gross wages	Employer NIC	Net wages	Deductions
Nominal ledger • Dr Wages and salaries expense account • Cr Wages and salaries control account (payable account)	**Nominal ledger** • Dr Wages and salaries expense account • Cr Wages and salaries control account (payable account)	**Nominal ledger** Records double entry of: • Dr Wages and salaries control account • Cr Bank account	**Nominal ledger** Records double entry of: • Dr Wages and salaries control account • Cr Payable account for each agency – for later payment

Overall effect:

- Wages and salaries control account has zero balance.
- Wages and salaries expense account shows total wages/salary cost including employer's NIC.
- Bank account pays net salaries and all deductions to appropriate agencies.

Exam focus

Ensure you understand the different methods of calculating gross wages and salaries. Worked examples are included in the study text if you need them.

chapter 8

Bank reconciliations

In this chapter

- Need for bank reconciliation.
- Preparing a bank reconciliation.
- Example bank reconciliation.

Need for bank reconciliation

Bank reconciliation needed to:
- Check accuracy of the cash book by agreeing balance to independent source.
- Identify cash book error = Entering receipt or payment incorrect (wrong amount).
- Identify cash book omissions = Items on bank statement not yet in cash book.

Reasons for cash book omissions include:

Item	Explanation
Dishonoured cheques	Customer's bank does not honour cheque (normally due to insufficient funds in customer account)
Credit transfers	Customer paying direct to company's bank account
Direct debit	Actual amount of direct debit not known until after it has occurred
Bank charges	Notified by bank in arrears

- Bank reconciliation explains difference between balance shown in cash book and balance shown on bank statement.
- Produced after most errors and omissions above have been rectified.

Main reconciling items are then:

Item	Explanation
Cheque payment	Delay between sending cheque to supplier and supplier banking cheque
Deposits	Delay between entering deposit in cash book and deposit clearing the bank

Preparing a bank reconciliation

- Sequence of preparation shown on diagram.
- In step 2, matching items normally evidenced by ticking the cash book and bank statement.
- In step 2, the previous bank reconciliation is needed to identify items entered in the cash book in March that did not clear the bank until April (as shown on the next reconciliation).

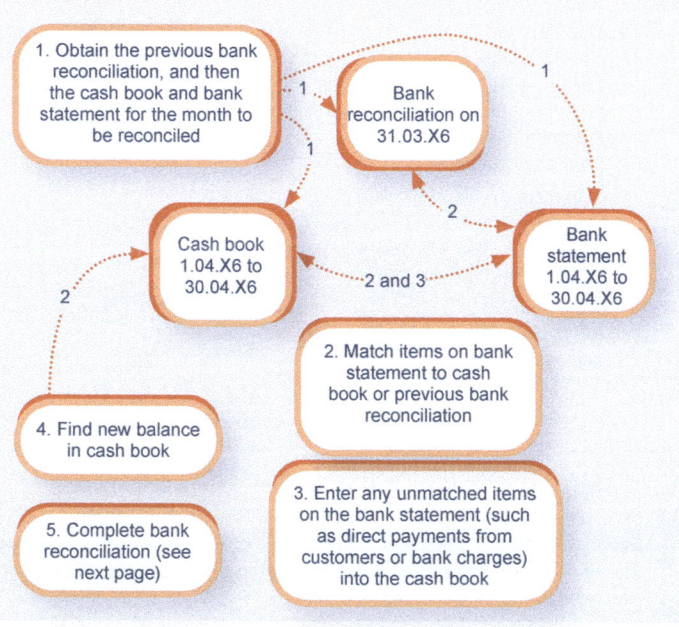

1. Obtain the previous bank reconciliation, and then the cash book and bank statement for the month to be reconciled

Bank reconciliation on 31.03.X6

Cash book 1.04.X6 to 30.04.X6

Bank statement 1.04.X6 to 30.04.X6

2. Match items on bank statement to cash book or previous bank reconciliation

3. Enter any unmatched items on the bank statement (such as direct payments from customers or bank charges) into the cash book

4. Find new balance in cash book

5. Complete bank reconciliation (see next page)

Bank reconciliations

Example bank reconciliation

- Unpresented cheques are payments in cash book but not yet at the bank. Deducted from bank balance.

- Outstanding lodgements are deposits in cash book but again not yet at the bank. Added to bank balance.

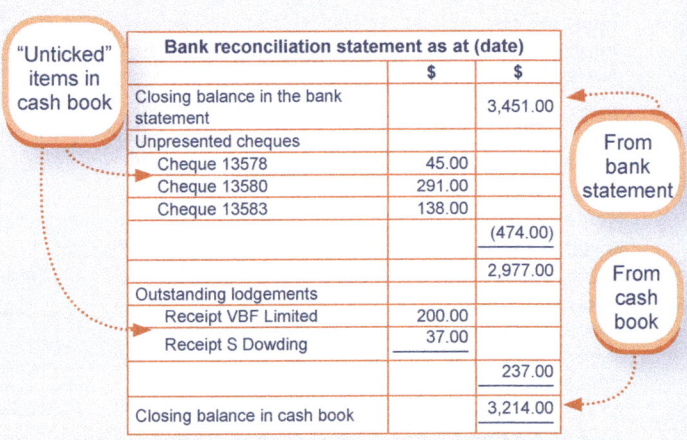

"Unticked" items in cash book

From bank statement

From cash book

Bank reconciliation statement as at (date)		
	$	$
Closing balance in the bank statement		3,451.00
Unpresented cheques		
Cheque 13578	45.00	
Cheque 13580	291.00	
Cheque 13583	138.00	
		(474.00)
		2,977.00
Outstanding lodgements		
Receipt VBF Limited	200.00	
Receipt S Dowding	37.00	
		237.00
Closing balance in cash book		3,214.00

Exam focus

Most examination questions in this area focus on explaining reconciling items on a reconciliation and finding new cash book balances. Ensure you can identify reconciling items and calculate revised cash book balances.

chapter 9

Control accounts

In this chapter

- Control account preparation.
- Receivables ledger control account preparation.
- Payables ledger control account preparation.
- Reasons for preparing control accounts.
- Discrepancies identified in the RLCA reconciliation.
- Discrepancies identified in the PLCA reconciliation.
- Format of reconciliation.

Control account preparation

The process is almost the same for both the sales and purchase ledgers.

Receivables ledger control account	Payables ledger control account
1. Write up the books of prime entry (sales day book, sales returns day book and cash receipts book)	1. Write up the books of prime entry (purchase day book, purchase returns day book and cash payments book)
2. Post totals to the RLCA	2. Post totals to the PLCA
3. Post individual amounts to the customer accounts in the receivables ledger	3. Post individual amounts to the supplier accounts in the purchase ledger
4. Find the closing balance on the RLCA	4. Find the closing balance on the PLCA
5. Find closing balances on the individual ledger accounts	5. Find closing balances on the individual ledger accounts
6. List closing balances on individual ledger accounts	6. List closing balances on individual ledger accounts
7. Compare total to RLCA total – should be the same	7. Compare total to PLCA total – should be the same

Also shown as a diagram on the next two pages. Black numbers on the diagrams refer to the steps above.

Definition

Control accounts are ledger accounts containing totals of a number of transactions.

Chapter 9

Receivables ledger control account preparation

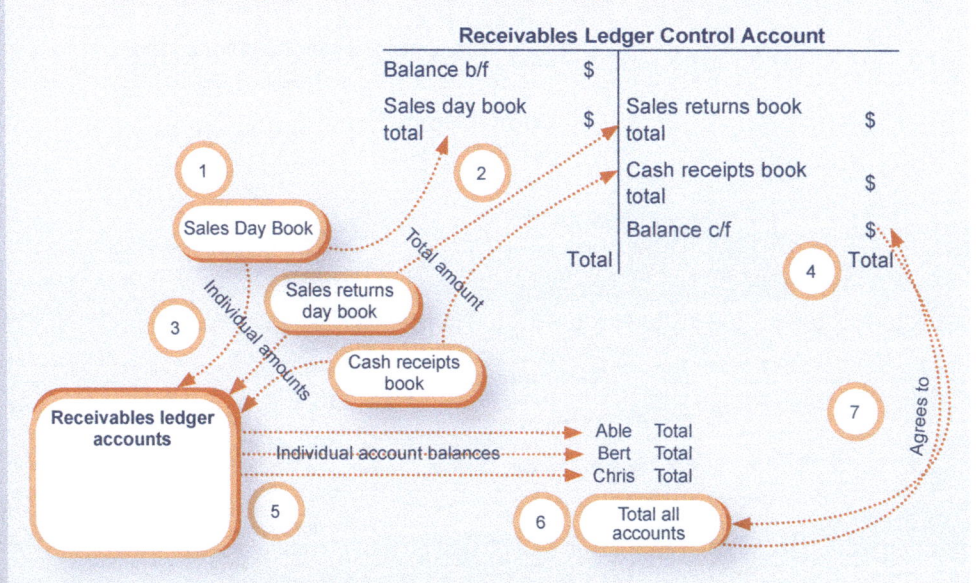

Receivables Ledger Control Account

Balance b/f	$		
Sales day book total	$	Sales returns book total	$
		Cash receipts book total	$
		Balance c/f	$
Total		Total	

1. Sales Day Book
2. Total amount
3. Individual amounts → Receivables ledger accounts
   - Sales returns day book
   - Cash receipts book
4. Total
5. Individual account balances → Able Total, Bert Total, Chris Total
6. Total all accounts
7. Agrees to

KAPLAN PUBLISHING

81

Control accounts

Payables ledger control account preparation

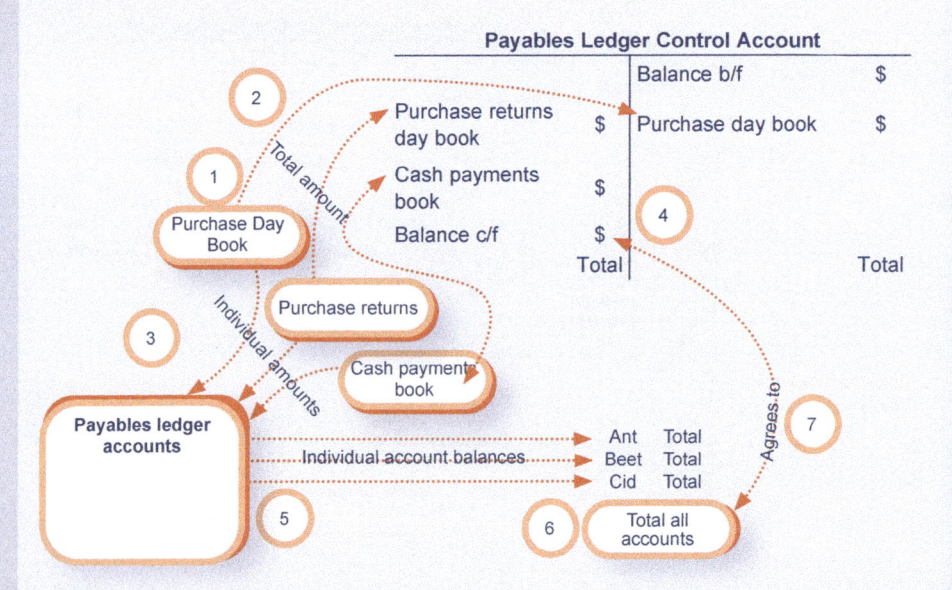

Payables Ledger Control Account

Purchase returns day book	$	Balance b/f	$
Cash payments book	$	Purchase day book	$
Balance c/f	$		
Total		Total	

Steps:
1. Purchase Day Book
2. Total amounts
3. Individual amounts → Payables ledger accounts
4. (Control account totals)
5. Individual account balances → Ant Total, Beet Total, Cid Total
6. Total all accounts
7. Agrees to

Reasons for preparing control accounts

- Shows total amount of receivables and payables.
- Check accuracy of accounting records.
- Identify errors in accounting records.

Control accounts

Discrepancies identified in the RLCA reconciliation

Error	Effect	Correct by
Day books under/over cast.	Balance on the RLCA incorrect and will not agree to list of balances on reconciliation.	Amend relevant entry in RLCA by the amount of the error.
Amount in SDB copied incorrectly to individual account in sales ledger e.g. invoice for $280 entered as $820 in ledger.	List of receivables ledger balances incorrect and will not agree to RLCA.	Checking posting to individual accounts and correct wrong entry – in this case credit ledger account by ($820 – $280) $540.
Amount posted to wrong side of individual receivables ledger account e.g. sale posted to credit rather than debit.	List of receivables ledger balances incorrect and will not agree to RLCA.	Checking posting to individual accounts and correct wrong entry. In this case enter double the amount of the sale on the debit side of account.
Individual account omitted from list of balances.	Total of list of balances less than RLCA balance.	Check extraction of list of balances from receivables ledger and add missing balance.

Errors normally corrected using the journal

e.g. undercasting of SDB by £500 has journal entry of:	Dr RLCA	$500
	Cr Sales	$500

Discrepancies identified in the PLCA reconciliation

Errors are very similar to the RLCA.

Error	Effect	Correct by
Day books under/over cast.	Balance on the PCLA incorrect and will not agree to list of balances on reconciliation.	Amend relevant entry in PCLA by the amount of the error.
Amount in PDB copied incorrectly to individual account in payables ledger e.g. invoice for $280 entered as $820 in ledger.	List of payables ledger balances incorrect and will not agree to PCLA.	Checking posting to individual accounts and correct wrong entry – in this case debit ledger account by ($820 – $280) $540.
Amount posted to wrong side of individual payables ledger account e.g. purchase posted to debit rather than credit.	List of payables ledger balances incorrect and will not agree to PCLA.	Checking posting to individual accounts and correct wrong entry. In this case enter double the amount of the purchase on the credit side of account.
Individual account omitted from list of balances.	Total of list of balances less than PCLA balance.	Check extraction of list of balances from payables ledger and add missing balance.

Format of reconciliation

E.g. receivables ledger reconciliation

Receivables ledger control account

	$		$
Balance b/f	X		
Under/overcasting of day book	X	Under/overcasting of day book	X
		Balance c/f	X
	X		X
Revised balance b/f	X		

Reconciliation

	$
Total list of balances originally extracted from receivables ledger	X
Errors: Invoice incorrectly copied to receivables ledger	X/(X)
Amount posted to wrong side of receivables ledger account	X/(X)
Individual account omitted	X
Adjusted list of receivables ledger balances = revised balance on RLCA	X

Exam focus

Ensure you understand how control account reconciliations are produced and the types of errors that can be identified using control accounts. In examination questions, think carefully about the double entry to correct errors identified as it may be opposite to the 'normal' entry e.g. posting to the wrong side of a ledger account needs an adjustment of double the amount to the other side of the ledger account.

Control accounts

chapter
10

The trial balance

In this chapter

- Producing a trial balance.
- Errors in producing a trial balance.
- Errors identified by a trial balance.
- Errors not identified by a trial balance.
- The suspense account.
- Correcting errors – clearing suspense account.

The trial balance

Producing a trial balance

Key Point

- Starting point for the preparation of profit and loss account and statement of financial position.
- Shows current balances on all accounts – useful for management.
- Helps identify errors in accounting records.

Producing a trial balance

1. Balance all accounts in nominal ledger.
2. List balances of all accounts separating debit and credit balances as shown on right (some headings e.g. assets will have more than one entry in a 'real' trial balance).
3. Total debits and credits – they should be the same.
4. Where debits do not equal credits, investigate and find reason(s) for discrepancy.

Balances on a trial balance

	Dr	Cr
Assets	$	
Liabilities		$
Capital		$
Drawings (from capital)	$	
Income (sales)		$
Discounts received		$
Purchase returns		$
Expenses	$	
Sales returns	$	
Irrecoverable debts	$	
Should be the same!	**Total**	**Total**

Definition

Trial balance = list of balances extracted from the nominal ledger.

Errors in producing a trial balance

> **Key Point**

- Mistake in finding balance on account in nominal ledger.
- Mistake in drafting trial balance (e.g. account omitted from list of balances, or debit balance placed in credit column).

Errors identified by a trial balance

Error	Example
Amounts for one transaction recorded differently in two ledger accounts.	Motor vehicle purchase recorded as $10,500 debit in the motor vehicle account and $10,050 in the bank account.
Transaction recorded as two debits or credits rather than one debit and one credit.	Motor vehicle purchase recorded as a debit in the motor vehicle account and also a debit in the bank account.
Error of single entry.	Motor vehicle purchase recorded as a debit in the motor vehicle account. No other entry is made.

Errors identified by trial balance debit and credit totals being different.

The trial balance

Errors not identified by a trial balance

In all these examples, the trial balance 'balances' because debit and credit amounts in the nominal ledger are the same.

Error	Example
Error of commission Correct amount entered into wrong account.	Sales invoice for D.Kay entered as debit in ledger account for K.Dee. Correct by credit to K.Dee's account and debit to D.Kay's account.
Error of principle Correct amount entered but in wrong 'class' of account.	Amount for a motor vehicle repair entered as a debit in motor vehicle account (treating the expense as an asset addition). Correct by credit to motor vehicle account and debit to motor vehicle repairs account.
Error of omission Transaction not recorded in the accounts at all.	Purchase invoice omitted from accounts. Correct by entering invoice into accounts.
Transposition error Debit and credit amounts for one transaction entered incorrectly.	Sales invoice for $1,030 entered as $1,003 in both RLCA and sales accounts. Correct by debit of $27 to RLCA and credit of $27 to sales account.

Chapter 10

Error	Example
Compensating error One error cancelled by another of same amount.	Debit on rent account understated by $50, but debit on light and heat account overstated by $50. Correct by debit of $50 to rent account and credit of $50 to light and heat account.
Error of original entry Original transaction entered incorrectly into book of prime entry.	Purchase invoice for $560 entered as $580 in PDB and then into PLCA and purchases account as $580. Correct by debit to PLCA and credit to purchases account of $20.
Complete reversal of entries Debit entered as credit and visa versa.	Cash sale recorded as debit to sales account and credit to bank account. Correct by debit to bank and credit to sales account for double the amount of the sale.

Exam focus

Ensure that you know what types of error affect the trial balance, and what types do not. Exam questions may explicitly ask you to distinguish these, or you may need to know for the purpose of correcting a suspense account.

The suspense account

Key Point

- Used when debits and credits in trial balance are not equal.
- Balance on suspense account = difference between debits and credits in trial balance.
- Trial balance therefore 'balances' by including the suspense account in list of balances.
- If have suspense account, next activity is to clear that account.

Correcting errors – clearing suspense account

Type of error	How to clear
Error causes an imbalance between debits and credits in accounts e.g. amount for one transaction recorded differently in two ledger accounts.	1. Identify ledger accounts affected. 2. Identify which ledger account(s) have incorrect balances. 3. Determine the amount of the error. 4. Determine whether a debit or credit is needed to clear the error. 5. Enter a corresponding debit or credit in the suspense account to complete the double entry correcting the initial error. 6. Ensure that the correcting entry is recorded in the Journal.
Error does not cause an imbalance between debits and credits in accounts e.g. it is an error of commission or omission.	1. Correct the error as outlined in the section on 'errors not identified by the trial balance' earlier in this section. 2. Remember that the suspense account will not be affected by this amendment. 3. Ensure that the double entry is recorded in the Journal.

Search for errors continues until the suspense account has a zero balance.

The trial balance

Exam focus

Some of the hardest examination questions involve the clearing of a suspense account balance. Try to follow the procedures outlined above for each error found, being very careful to get the debits and credit of the correcting entry right. There is a worked example in the study text if you need practise in this area.

Index

Index

A

Accounting for payroll 73
Accounting systems 3
Accounts and ledgers 12
Aged payables analysis 43
Aged receivables analysis 30
Authorising and coding of purchase invoices 36

B

Balancing accounts 14
Balancing supplier accounts 41
Bank-customer relationship 51
Basic pay calculations 70
Books of prime entry 12

C

Capital and revenue expenditure 15
Cash payments 49
Checking purchase invoices and credit notes 35
Clearing of cheques 52
Communications with customers 31
Communications with suppliers 43
Computerised accounting 15
Contactless payments 56
Control account preparation 80
Correcting errors – clearing suspense account 95
Credit and debit cards 55

D

Discounts 22
Discrepancies identified in the PLCA reconciliation 85
Discrepancies identified in the RLCA reconciliation 84
Double-entry bookkeeping 13

Index

E

Errors in producing a trial balance 91
Errors not identified by a trial balance 92

I

Irrecoverable debts 32

L

Limited company 2

M

Making a petty cash claim 60

N

Need for bank reconciliation 76

O

Other business documents 8
Overtime, bonuses and commission 71

P

Partnership 2
Payables ledger control account preparation 82
Preparing a bank reconciliation 77
Preparing a sales invoice 25
Producing a trial balance 90

R

Receivables ledger control account preparation 81
Reconciling petty cash 65
Recording a sales invoice 26
Recording of petty cash 62
Recording purchase returns 39

Index

Recording purchases 37
Recording receipts 46
Recording sales returns 28
Reimbursement of petty cash 64

S

Sales/purchases systems 6
Sales tax 20
Sole trader 2
Statements of account 30
Supplier statements 42

T

The accounting equation 10
The suspense account 94
Types of business 2

V

Variable consideration 23

W

Wages/salaries system 68